GENTLEMAN'S ATTRACTIVENESS

HOW TO BE AN ATTRACTIVE MAN

For Andriana

Where does the attractiveness come from?

At the beginning, it is worth emphasizing that the phenomenon of attractiveness itself has several solid sources - the most important of them is evolution.

Moreover, attractiveness also results from cultural factors, but also by pure chance.

Consequently, women are attracted to physical strength, good health, social position and compliance with the framework of applicable social norms.

It is work on these elements that allows us to improve our attractiveness!

Why is it worth taking care of your attractiveness?

Not every man is born handsome, but everyone can make themselves attractive! Why is it worth it?

Attractiveness has a huge impact on many elementary aspects of everyday reality - personal, but also social and even professional. Just a few simple tricks and methods are enough to significantly improve our image!

Not everyone is handsome, but everyone can be attractive!

Being attractive and being handsome are completely different concepts.

Being handsome means external qualities that refer to a person's outward appearance. It may include, for example, facial symmetry, i.e. aspects that we have no influence on.

Attractiveness is a more complex category that can include both physical characteristics and personality traits. In addition to appearance, attractiveness can also be related to self-confidence, sense of humor, intelligence, empathy and other qualities that we can work on.

Why is it worth caring about attractiveness?

So, what are the most important benefits of caring for attractiveness? Here are the reasons why it is worth taking care of this component of men's reality:

1. Boost your self-confidence: Looking and feeling attractive can significantly impact your self-confidence. People who feel attractive are usually more self-confident, which can help them achieve their goals - both in their personal and professional lives.

2. Positive First Impression: First impressions are extremely important. Looking attractive can help you make a positive impression on others, which can be beneficial in many situations such as job interviews, business meetings, or meetings.

3. Healthy lifestyle: Taking care of your attractiveness often means taking care of your health. People who try to look attractive usually lead a healthier lifestyle, paying attention to a proper diet, regular physical activity and sleep.

4. Kinder interpersonal relationships: Attractiveness can help you build better interpersonal relationships. People are often more willing to establish contacts and cooperate with people who seem attractive and well-groomed.

5. Impact on well-being: By taking care of yourself and your appearance, you can improve your overall well-being. Staying attractive can help prevent stress and other health problems.

6. Inspiration to others: People who strive to look attractive are often an inspiration to others. They can motivate others to take care of themselves and make healthier choices.

7. Positive impact on career: In some professions and industries, attractiveness can have an impact on career success. Although competence is definitely more important, attractiveness can help attract the attention of employers or clients.

The most important rule - act!

However, there is a lot of work ahead of you to achieve this! Attractiveness is the result of regularity, consistency and discipline. With each passing day, the changes you make will become easier and easier to implement, until you build a completely new routine.

This book is a collection of specially selected tips for specific visual areas. Start reading from the very beginning or choose a specific section and then implement the techniques that work for you.

Here it's time to say goodbye.

Because by the end of this guide, you will be a completely different person.

You will be a Gentleman!

1. Follow the routine

Maintaining proper hygiene requires systematic action immediately after waking up and before going to sleep, Create two routines - morning and evening.

2. Morning routine

There are a few particularly important steps when implementing your morning routine:

- Take a cold shower.
- Wash your face.
- Apply vitamin C serum.
- Wash it to.
- Apply a cream with SPF.

3. Evening routine

There are a few particularly important steps when implementing your evening routine:

- Take a shower.
- Wash your face.
- Wash it to.
- Apply a cream with retinol.

4. Use serum with vitamin c

Vitamin C is a strong antioxidant that helps fight harmful free radicals produced in the skin by UV rays, environmental pollutants and other factors.

Regular use of vitamin C serum can help maintain healthy, radiant and youthful skin, improving its overall condition and condition.

Using the serum is part of the morning routine.

5. Take a shower every day

Taking a shower daily is a basic element of personal hygiene that helps keep the body clean, getting rid of dirt, sweat and other unpleasant odors. Body odor can have a big impact on your first impression, so it's important to keep your skin fresh and clean.

Washing your body regularly while showering helps keep your skin healthy by removing dead skin cells and dirt. Maintaining healthy skin can improve its appearance and elasticity, which can further improve a man's attractiveness.

To sum up, taking a shower every day is an important element of personal hygiene that can influence a man's attractiveness by keeping his skin clean, fresh and healthy, increasing his self-confidence and managing body odor.

6. Take care of your breathe

Fresh breath plays an important role in everyday social interaction and influences the overall impression we make on other people.

Fresh breath is a key element of the first impression you make on other people. Bad breath can be off-putting and make social interactions uncomfortable for both parties.

Keeping your breath fresh can increase your confidence in everyday interactions because you don't have to worry about potentially unpleasant breath odor.

Oral health is crucial to the overall health of the body. Bad breath may be the result of health problems, bacteria, or dental problems.

How to prevent this?

- Regular oral hygiene: Brushing your teeth regularly at least twice a day, using dental floss and mouthwash, and cleaning your tongue helps remove bacteria and food particles that can cause bad breath.

- Avoiding strong-smelling foods: Some foods, such as onions, garlic and spices, can leave a strong odor in the mouth. Using sugar-free chewing gum or rinsing your mouth after consuming such products may help alleviate this problem.

- Regular visits to the dentist: Regular visits to the dentist help maintain your oral health and detect and treat any tooth and gum problems that may lead to bad breath.

7. Use deodorant

Underarm deodorant is one of the essential personal care products that helps you stay fresh all day long.

The main function of a deodorant is to prevent unpleasant odors caused by bacteria growing on the skin under the arms. Deodorants contain ingredients that inhibit the growth of bacteria and neutralize the odor of sweat.

It is worth paying attention to the ingredients contained in the deodorant, especially if you are prone to allergies or skin irritations. Some deodorants may contain fragrances, alcohol, parabens or aluminum salts, which may cause allergic reactions in some people.

Many deodorants have additional fragrance properties that leave a pleasant aroma on the skin. The choice of fragrance depends on individual preferences, although it is worth remembering that some strongly scented deodorants may mix with the natural scent of perfumes or body creams.

8. Trim your nails regularly

Trimming your nails regularly has many health and hygiene benefits and can also impact the overall appearance of your hands and feet.

Shortly cut nails look neater and more aesthetic than long and untrimmed ones.

Shortly cut nails are easier to keep clean and hygienic because bacteria and dirt do not accumulate under them as easily as under long nails.

To sum up, trimming your nails regularly is important for maintaining health, hygiene and aesthetics.

9. Take care of the smell

Choosing the perfect perfume scent can have a significant impact on our well-being, appearance and overall self-confidence.

The scent of perfume can be an expression of our personality and lifestyle. By choosing perfumes that match our fragrance preferences, we can express our individuality and uniqueness.

A well-chosen scent can increase our attractiveness in the eyes of other people. The scent of perfume may be subtle, but it can attract attention and evoke positive reactions.

The scent of perfume can complement the overall styling. By choosing a fragrance that suits our outfit and situation, we create a complete and coherent image.

What's more, nowadays there are many opportunities to design your own fragrance!

10. Use natural products

Natural products often contain plant-based ingredients that are gentle on the skin and body. They do not contain artificial dyes, preservatives or other harmful chemicals that may cause skin irritation or allergies.

Natural ingredients, such as vegetable oils, herbal extracts and shea butter, have soothing, moisturizing and nourishing properties for the skin. They can help maintain its proper hydration, elasticity and healthy appearance.

To sum up, using natural products can bring many benefits to your health, the environment and your local community. Therefore, it is worth considering choosing natural products as part of your daily care and self-care.

11. Use a facial brush

The facial brush not only cleans the facial surface but also stimulates circulation.

12. Use matching creams

Men's facial skin may be particularly susceptible to dryness due to daily shaving. Using moisturizing creams helps maintain the appropriate level of skin hydration, preventing it from drying out and flaking.

Facial skin is exposed to harmful external factors, such as UV radiation, environmental pollution, wind and frost. Facial creams may contain protective ingredients such as sunscreens, antioxidants and moisturizers that protect the skin from harmful environmental influences.

There are four basic skin types - dry skin, normal skin, combination skin and oily skin.

If you have trouble identifying your type, take a virtual test or contact an expert.

13. Use cream with filter

The effect of the first impression is inextricably linked to our face. That's why you need to take proper care of this area of attractiveness. How?

It is worth mentioning two terms here - UVB and UVA.

The first one is especially dangerous during holidays and is responsible for burns. The second one shows constant activity and causes wrinkles and even the extremely dangerous process of photoaging of the skin and other diseases!

For this reason, it is worth remembering about an effective sunscreen. What does this mean in practice?

When choosing the perfect cosmetic, you should pay attention to the SPF value - Sun Protection Factor. This is an international symbol that allows you to determine the scope of protection against UVB rays. An SPF value of 30 provides high and very high protection, so we should use such products.

Care should cover the entire face, but also the ears and neck!

14. Use retinol

It is also worth using appropriate cosmetics at night. Here, we recommend retinol serum, which is a very effective skin care product.

Regular use of retinol can help improve the overall appearance of your skin, giving it a healthier, more radiant and younger appearance.

Include this item in your evening routine.

15. Darken your skin

Darker skin can be made to increase the attractiveness of any man. However, there is a way to take care of your attractive skin color naturally.

For this purpose, it is worth consuming products rich in beta-carotene, which causes a slight change in the color of our skin.

Ingredients containing beta-carotene include carrots, apricots, melon, mango or sweet potatoes. However, the diet should be balanced and healthy.

16. Use a dermaroller

This small mesotherapy device promotes the regeneration and reconstruction of the skin itself.

The resulting micro-damages activate the formation of collagen and elastin, and increase the absorption of all creams and substances.

17. Use a facial roller

This intuitive roller increases skin firmness, stimulates circulation, helps remove toxins and reduces swelling.

Massage should be done every day. It is recommended to use sliding movements, from the center of the face outwards

18. Apply a cooling mask

Completing your morning chores is a great time to put on a special cooling mask. The mask does not limit visibility and allows for quick reduction of all types of swelling.

To do this, just leave the mask in the fridge and apply it to your face in the morning.

The professional mask can also be heated, which promotes evening relaxation.

19. Practice facial yoga

Facial yoga, like other forms of physical exercise, can provide many health benefits, regardless of gender.

Facial exercises such as massage and muscle stretching can stimulate blood circulation, which can help improve skin health and overall appearance.

Facial yoga exercises can help you become aware of facial muscle movements, which leads to better control of your facial expressions and emotional expression.

20. Shave your private parts

Shaving intimate areas may simply look aesthetically pleasing and be perceived as more neat and attractive.

Shaving your intimate areas can make maintaining hygiene easier because shorter or hairless areas are easier to wash and keep clean. This may also reduce the risk of unpleasant odors.

What's more, this procedure makes the male penis appear larger!

21. Goal shoulders

Smooth skin on the back looks more aesthetic and attractive. Shaving can help you maintain a neat and well-groomed appearance.

Shaving your back can make it easier to maintain hygiene because the skin is easier to clean and keep clean, and it can also reduce the risk of unpleasant odors.

22. Take care of your eyebrows

Taking care of your eyebrows is not just for women. Men can and should also pay attention to the appearance and care of their eyebrows.

Well-groomed eyebrows can improve the overall appearance of your face and give it a more defined shape. Attention to details, such as the shape of the eyebrows, can make the face appear more structured and attractive.

Eyebrows influence facial expression. Well-shaped eyebrows can help define your eyes, giving your face a more expressive character. This can also affect how we are perceived by others.

User manual:

- The regulation itself is an individual matter and should be tailored to the characteristics of the guy. The entire procedure should only emphasize the shape of the eyebrows.

- Place in front of a mirror in a brightly lit place and use the eyebrow shaping tool kit.

- Decide what eyebrow shape you would like to achieve. Do you just want to trim the longer hairs or maybe you want to give your eyebrows a more defined shape.

- Use eyebrow tweezers to remove individual, unwanted hairs between the eyebrows and under the eyebrow arch. Avoid over-removing to maintain a natural look.

- After shaping your eyebrows, apply a mild moisturizing cream or a special balm to care for the skin around the eyebrows.

23. Take care of your teeth

Keeping your teeth healthy and white is important for many reasons, both in terms of physical and mental health.

Remember to visit the dentist at least twice a year.

Regular dental care and dental care can help you avoid more serious problems that require long-term and expensive treatment. Prevention is usually more cost-effective and saves time and money.

Healthy teeth are crucial to overall oral health. Poor oral hygiene can lead to problems such as tooth decay, gum disease and even tooth loss. Regular brushing, flossing and visiting the dentist help keep your teeth healthy.

White, healthy teeth are important for everyday functioning. Maintaining an aesthetically pleasing smile can improve our self-confidence and positively impact our social and professional relationships.

An aesthetic smile can attract attention and make a person seem more attractive to others. An attractive smile can influence your perception in a business context. In some professions, especially those that require direct contact with people, an aesthetic smile may be considered an asset, having a positive impact on your professional career.

DAILY ROUTINE:

- 2 x brushing x 3 minutes

- flossing
- rinsing

24. Take care of your feet

Well-groomed feet are one of the elements of caring for your appearance and personal hygiene. Clean, trimmed nails, smooth skin and no signs of skin disease contribute to an overall positive impression.

By taking care of his feet, a man can express concern for himself and his health. This may be perceived as an element of concern for one's appearance, which affects the overall impression of a well-groomed man.

How to take care of your feet?

- Regular hygiene: Wash your feet daily using warm water and mild soap. Try to thoroughly clean the spaces between your toes.

- Drying your feet: After washing, dry your feet carefully, especially between the toes. A humid environment may favor the growth of fungi.

- Trimming your nails: Trim your nails regularly to keep them short and in shape. Remember to cut straight and avoid rounding to prevent ingrown toenails.

- Skin care: Apply a moisturizing foot cream, especially to areas prone to dryness. Concentrate on the heels and sides of your feet. If the skin is thickened, you can use a foot file or a pumice stone.

• Wearing comfortable shoes: Choose shoes made of breathable materials that ensure adequate air circulation. Avoid wearing shoes that are too tight to avoid abrasions and blisters.

• Using insoles: If you need additional support or suffer from arch problems, consider using orthopedic insoles.

• Avoid walking barefoot in public places: To minimize the risk of infection with fungal infections or viruses, avoid walking barefoot in public places such as swimming pools or locker rooms.

25. Take care of your hands

Taking care of your hands is important for every person, regardless of gender.

Hands are often one of the first things we notice when meeting someone new. Well-groomed hands can create a positive first impression, emphasizing care for yourself and your appearance.

Well-groomed hands can make a man feel confident and attractive. The skin on your hands, nails and the shape of your fingers can be an important part of the overall impression you make on others.

Regular hand skin care, nail clipping and skin moisturization are the basic activities that will help keep your hands in good condition and emphasize their attractiveness.

26. Trim your nose hair

Nose hairs are responsible for keeping dust, bacteria and other microorganisms from entering the respiratory system. However, excessive hair can cause dirt to become trapped, which can lead to infection. Removing excess hair can help keep your nose clean.

Removing nose hair is also a matter of aesthetics. Regular removal of excess nose hair ensures a pleasant, tidy and aesthetic appearance.

It's worth adding this element to our weekly aesthetic maintenance schedule.

27. Wash your face with cold water

Starting the day with contact with cold water generates many benefits for our skin,

- Improved circulation: Cold water stimulates blood circulation in the skin, which can make the face brighter and more radiant.

- Reduce puffiness: The cool temperature of the water can help reduce puffiness, especially under the eyes, which can be especially beneficial after nighttime.

- Pore Reduction: Cold water can temporarily shrink the skin's enlarged pores, giving the skin a smoother appearance.

- Cleanse your skin: Cold water can help remove excess natural skin oil and impurities, which can help keep your skin clean.

- Strengthen the skin: Cold water exposure can stimulate the skin to produce collagen, which may help maintain its elasticity.

- Invigorating and energizing: Cool water can also be invigorating and stimulating, which can be useful especially in the morning to help wake up and improve energy.

28. Don't touch your face

Constantly touching your face can have a number of negative consequences for your skin and health. Here are some reasons why you shouldn't do this:

• Transferring bacteria: Touching your face, especially with dirty hands, can transfer bacteria from your hands to your skin, increasing the risk of infection and acne.

• Worsening the skin condition: Touching your face, especially in the acne area, can aggravate the skin condition. Transferring bacteria and manipulating the skin can lead to irritation, redness and blackheads.

• Damage to delicate skin: Facial skin is delicate and sensitive. Constant touching can cause damage, scratches and even contribute to premature aging of the skin.

• Transfer of pollutants: Touching your face can transfer pollutants from the environment to your skin, which can lead to clogged pores and blackheads.

• Spreading infection: In times of infectious diseases such as flu or cold, frequent touching of the face with hands can increase the risk of spreading viruses to the mucous membranes of the nose, mouth and eyes, which increases the chances of getting sick.

● Disruption of the protective layer: The skin has a natural protective layer, and constant touching can disrupt this protection, leaving the skin more susceptible to infection and irritation.

Be more aware of your face touching habits. Being aware of this action can help you identify times when you may be unconsciously touching your face and work on changing these habits.

29. Hunter's eyes

The hunter's eyes are almond-shaped eyes that are set deep in the skull. They are usually protected by a prominent brow bone. According to the concept of hunter's eyes, the center of the eye is horizontally wide, vertically narrow and directed upwards. The upper edge of the pupil is in line with the lower fold of the eyelid, and the lower edge is below it.

THERE ARE SEVERAL CHARACTERISTICS of hunter's eyes that make them attractive:

Self-confidence: The eyes of a hunter exude a sense of control and assertiveness, which are very desirable qualities in a partner. Direct eye contact is the hallmark of a hunter's eyes and communicates a sense of security and reliability.

Power: A hunter's eyes communicate a sense of power and authority. Hunter eyes are shaped upwards, giving them a piercing and focused gaze that can be unsettling.

Focus: The hunter's eyes have a great intensity that can be both attractive and overwhelming upon first contact.

How to get hunter's eyes?

Through mewing exercises!

Mewing is a phrase commonly used to describe a set of exercises designed to improve jaw posture by properly positioning the tongue in the mouth. Some people believe that these exercises can change the shape of the face.

Instructions: To perform the exercise, close your mouth and place your teeth so that they are slightly touching. Then move your tongue up and apply light pressure. There should be a slight pressure throughout the entire jaw. It is important that this exercise does not block the airway while breathing. Try to hold this position for as long as possible during the day.

30. Full eyes

Full and visible eyes increase a man's attractiveness. To achieve this, avoid squinting.

31. Take care of your posture

Correct posture supports spine health. Maintaining the natural curvature of the spine helps distribute the load evenly among the vertebrae, joints and muscles, which prevents discs and back pain.

Poor posture can lead to various ailments such as back pain, neck pain, and even headaches. Improving your posture can bring relief and reduce pain.

Correct posture affects the overall appearance of the body. A person who keeps their back straight and avoids curvature looks more confident and attractive.

People who maintain good posture often experience improved overall well-being. Improving circulation, providing adequate amounts of oxygen to the body and reducing pain contribute to better mental well-being.

How to achieve this?

- Pay attention to your body posture. Sometimes people don't realize that they have bad posture. Regularly check whether you maintain the natural curvature of your spine when standing or sitting.

- Good posture starts with the legs. Make sure your feet are evenly weighted and your body weight is distributed evenly on both legs. Avoid putting your weight on one leg.

● Regular stretching and exercise can help keep your muscles flexible, making it easier to maintain a straight posture.

32. Get rid of the "belly"

Getting rid of your "beer belly," which is the fat that accumulates around your belly area, can be beneficial to your physical and mental health.

Reducing abdominal fat contributes to overall health improvement. This can lower cholesterol levels, blood pressure and reduce the risk of many chronic diseases.

Regular physical activity and a healthy diet, which are often part of the fat reduction process, contribute to overall improvement in physical condition. Strengthening your abdominal muscles can also improve your posture.

Losing excess fat can have a positive impact on your self-esteem and self-confidence. People who make efforts to reduce fat often experience improved mood and overall well-being.

How to achieve this?

- Focus on a healthy and balanced diet. Limit your calorie intake, avoid processed foods, fatty foods and sweets. Instead, choose wholesome products!

- Regular exercise is key to reducing fat. Focus on cardio workouts such as running, swimming, cycling or aerobic exercises to burn calories. Additionally, include exercises that strengthen your abdominal muscles, such as planks, crunches or leg raises, in your training plan.

33. Build broad shoulders

Taking care of broad shoulders has its benefits from both a health and aesthetic perspective.

Broad shoulders give the figure an athletic look, which is desirable from an aesthetic point of view. Developed shoulders can also help create body proportions, which has a positive effect on your overall appearance.

Strengthening your shoulders helps increase the overall strength of your arms and chest. This is crucial, both for athletes and people leading an active lifestyle. Broad shoulders are crucial for performing many daily activities, such as lifting heavy objects.

How to achieve this?

- Pull-ups: This is an excellent exercise for developing your back and shoulder muscles.

- Overhead Barbell Press: Focus on this technique to activate your shoulder muscles.

- Dumbbell Side Raise: This exercise isolates the lateral shoulder muscles.

34. Take care of your hair

This chapter concerns visual aspects and proper care of our hair. Here are some universal tips:

- Wash your hair regularly, but avoid over-washing, which can over-remove your scalp's natural oils.

- Use mild shampoos and conditioners adapted to your hair type.

- Avoid rubbing your hair vigorously with a towel after washing. It is better to gently squeeze out the moisture and use a towel made of soft material.

- Use gentle brushes and combs to avoid hair breakage.

- Trimming the ends every few months helps keep your hair healthy by eliminating split ends and improving its overall appearance.

- If you spend a lot of time in the sun, protect your hair from harmful UV rays by wearing a hat or using products with a UV filter.

- Include nutrients in your diet such as vitamins, minerals and protein that support hair health.

- Stress can negatively affect the condition of your hair.

35. Choose the right hairstyle

Choosing a hairstyle depends on many factors such as face shape, hair texture, lifestyle, aesthetic preferences and much more. Choose hair styles that compliment your face shape:

- For a round face: sides and bottom cut short; Quiff, Pompadour, Brush Back, Comb over.

- For an oval face: Most hair styles suit an oval face.

- For a square face: short styles; Pompadour.

- For a triangular face: large volume; Quiff.

- For a diamond face: longer hair, messy style.

- For oblong faces: longer hairstyles that complement the sides.

Make sure the style you choose takes into account the structure of your hair. Some hairstyles work better with smooth hair, while others may benefit from natural waves or curly strands.

Choose hairstyles that suit your lifestyle. If you have an active lifestyle, make sure your hair is easy to maintain and style.

Don't be afraid of baldness! Baldness can be very attractive, and many people consider it a feature of self-confidence and masculinity. Baldness can give a man a unique and distinctive appearance.

Combined with the right style of clothing, it can be a strong styling element.

During the first signs of baldness, it is worth remembering to keep your hair neat and short, and maybe even a new ritual with the barber's razor.

36. Choose the right beard style

Your beard style can be a form of expressing your identity and lifestyle.

A properly selected beard style can help balance the proportions of the face, highlight its strengths and hide any imperfections.

Well-groomed and properly styled beards can make you appear more confident and well-groomed. At the same time, facial hair can help hide certain skin imperfections, scars or facial asymmetry.

WHAT IS THE PROCESS of choosing the perfect facial hair?

- Determine the shape of your face.

- Determine the thickness of your beard.

- Browse through different beard styles.

- Choose the beard style that best suits your face shape and hair thickness.

37. Know your face shape

A round face:

- ○ Round cheeks and jaw.
- ○ The forehead is low and the hairline is rounded.

Square face:

- ○ Forehead, cheeks and jaw of equal length.
- ○ Prominent chin.
- ○ Square hairline.
- ○ The forehead is low and wide.
- ○ The width and height of the face are similar in size.

Triangular face:

- ○ The high forehead is the widest point of the face.
- ○ Pointy beard.
- ○ V shape

Oval face:

- ○ Similar height of forehead, nose and chin.
- ○ Cheekbones as the widest point.
- ○ The chin is slightly narrowed.

Rectangular face:

○ Oblong cheeks.
○ Scratched beard.
○ Jaw, forehead and cheeks of similar width.

Diamond Face:

○ Prominent cheekbones as the widest point of the face.
○ Pointy chin.
○ Cheeks wider than forehead.

38. Think about a beard

A beard can add character and a masculine expression to your face. It can also help you express your own style and individuality. A well-chosen beard can be a fashionable element of men's styling that increases attractiveness.

For some men, wearing a beard can be a source of greater self-confidence and masculinity. This may have a positive impact on their well-being and self-perception.

39. Match your facial hair to your face

Around face:

  ○ Facial slimming.
  ○ The line of facial hair along the cheekbones with a longer
bottom.

Square face:

  ○ Any type with square edges.
  ○ Goatee.

Triangular face:

  ○ Beard that is opposite to the shape of the face.
  ○ Lush facial hair on and under the cheeks.
  ○ Rectangular shape,

Oval face:

  ○ Universal shape.
  ○ Any type of beard.

Rectangular face:

  ○ Optical shortening of the face.
  ○ Short stubble.

Diamond face:

○ Rounded stubble covering the entire face.

40. Stimulate your hair

For many people, healthy, thick hair is perceived as attractive and is an element of external attractiveness. That's why many people take steps to improve the overall appearance of their hair.

Actions to stimulate hair growth can be taken to prevent or alleviate the process of baldness.

Ways to stimulate hair growth:

- healthy diet,
- proper care,
- natural supplementation.
- using lotions and oils,
- using hair scrub,
- avoiding negative conditions,
- head massage,
- stimulating circulation using a mesoroller.

41. Take advantage of the consultant's knowledge

Consulting services regarding our hair and beard do not require huge financial outlays.

The expert will analyze our face and then propose a solution tailored to our unique features, emphasizing certain features and reducing others.

Thanks to this, you will gain an original and unique style and clear instructions when visiting a barber or hairdresser.

42. Take care of your chin

The appearance of your chin can affect your overall personal image. For many men, it is important to feel confident and attractive, and the shape of the chin can be an important element of this image.

The shape of the chin affects the overall symmetry of the face. A symmetrical face is often considered more attractive from an aesthetic point of view, and proper care of the chin can help achieve harmony in facial proportions.

Ways to have an attractive chin:

• get yourself checked and see if your double chin is not the result of a disease.

• lose excess weight,

• take care of a proper diet,

• take care of the correct body position,

• pay attention to proper breathing,

• do facial yoga,

• perform facial massage, also using a gua sha stone.

If such methods do not bring results, there are still two options - covering the double chin with attractive facial hair and professional services from an aesthetic medicine doctor.

43. Choose the right glasses

If you wear glasses, it is worth adapting their style to your face. What does this mean in practice?

Glasses should be an element of your image that highlights your assets. A very good tip is the contrast rule, according to which the style of glasses should differ from the shape of our face.

Glasses should also match the actual dimensions of our face, emphasizing the color of our eyes or hair.

When choosing a glasses model, it is also worth remembering our wardrobe. By choosing a classic, yet elegant and minimalist style, we will ensure flexibility and timelessness.

Our glasses should always be clean and in good technical condition.

- Triangular face: rectangular, browline, oval, aviator, geometric, wrapped glasses

- Heart face: rectangular, aviator, geometric, wrapped glasses

- Diamond face: oval, aviator, round, wrapped glasses

- Round face: rectangular, square, aviator, wrapped glasses

- Oblong face: wayframe, browline, oval, aviator, round, geometric, geometric, intricate

- Oval face: rectangular, square, wayframe, browline, aviator, geometric, intricate glasses

- Square face: wayframe, browline, oval, aviator, round, intricate glasses

44. Take care of your wardrobe

The first impression is crucial, especially in the context of social meetings, dates or job interviews. A wardrobe can significantly influence the first impression, presenting a man as well-groomed, stylish and aware of his appearance.

Dressing in a way that makes a man feel good in his own skin can help to increase his self-confidence and positive attitude. A well-fitting wardrobe can emphasize the advantages of the figure and mask any imperfections.

The way a man dresses can be an expression of his personality and lifestyle. Properly selected clothes can help express individuality, interests and professionalism.

45. Find your style

Your dressing style can be an expression of your personality, interests, values and lifestyle. Finding your own style allows you to express yourself and show the world who you really are.

The one who has an individual style stands out in a crowd. Having your own recognizable style allows you to stand out and be remembered by others.

Once you have your own style defined, it becomes easier for you to make purchasing decisions. You avoid unnecessary spending on things that don't suit your style, and you save time by avoiding long hours spent looking for the right clothes.

46. Discover your figure

To do this, measure and record the following dimensions and then identify the one with the highest value:

- chest
- talia
- hips
- height below the rib line

Here are 4 types of construction

1. inverted triangle: broad shoulders, strong chest, narrow hips, strong legs, universal and desirable
2. pear shape: requires correcting the position and aligning the upper part of the body with the lower part
3. apple: proportional hips and shoulders, visible belly, clothes should fit the body, but not be tight
4. rectangle: the proportions of the waist and hip arms are similar, it is important to expose the waist and optically widen the shoulder line

47.Start with the basics

When assembling your outfit for a given day, start with the base, i.e. pants and a shirt, and then move on to all the additions and accessories.

48. Buy clothes that fit

Fitted clothes emphasize the figure better, which can make a man look more well-groomed and attractive.

When a man wears clothes that fit his figure perfectly, it can increase his self-confidence. By feeling good in their own skin, they can be more open and confident in contacts with others.

However, it is worth remembering that a man's attractiveness does not depend solely on his clothes. Other factors such as personality, character, sense of humor and intelligence also play an important role in overall attractiveness. Clothes are only one element of the entire image.

49. Show off your triceps

Wear T-shirts that show off your triceps or roll up your sleeves! Well-developed triceps can add physical attractiveness. Wearing shirts that highlight these muscles can help you put your best foot forward and attract other people's attention.

This treatment optically enlarges your muscles.

50. Match your outfit to the occasion

Matching clothes to the occasion is important because the right outfit can help express respect for a given situation, have a positive impact on the first impression and emphasize our personality and professionalism.

There are certain dress code expectations in some situations, such as at formal events, at work, at family gatherings, etc. Conforming to these standards shows respect for the occasion and for other people present.

Our clothes can influence how others perceive us. By choosing the right outfit, we can control the first impression other people make on us.

Make your outfit reflect the upcoming circumstances.

The style of a true gentleman does not mean an elegant, sophisticated wardrobe, but the ability to adapt it to the occasion,

51. Find the perfect jeans

Choosing the perfect jeans can be crucial for comfort and style while carrying out everyday duties.

Choose jeans that fit your body size. Make sure the pants fit well at the waist, hips and leg length. Avoid jeans that are too tight or too loose.

Choose jeans made of high-quality materials that are durable and comfortable. Good quality denim will wear well and will not wear out quickly.

Choose the jeans color that best suits your wardrobe and lifestyle. Classic colors such as navy blue, black or dark denim are usually the most universal and easy to combine with other clothes.

Choose the perfect cut:

- Straight - means straight legs along the entire length, which optically lengthens the limbs. Very comfortable and universal.

- Tapered - a cut that provides more room in the thighs, but tapers towards the legs.

- Slim - a model chosen especially by slim people. These jeans fit the figure, but do not tighten.

- Regular - a classic model with straight legs.

52. Choose quality

There are many reasons why it is worth investing in high-quality clothing.

High-quality clothing is usually made of better materials and higher production standards, which makes it more durable. By choosing high-quality clothing, you can be sure that it will last for a long time, which can ultimately save you money in the long run since you won't have to replace your clothes as often.

Clothing made of high-quality materials is often softer, gentle on the skin and more breathable than those made of cheaper materials. Wearing comfortable clothing can improve your well-being and comfort throughout the day.

Good quality materials also retain their shape and color even after many washes, which means your clothes look fresh and elegant for longer.

53. Do regular check-ups

Regularly checking and cleaning the wardrobe helps maintain order and space in the apartment. Getting rid of unused clothes allows you to avoid excessive clutter, which can have a positive impact on your well-being and the organization of your living space.

Getting rid of things we don't wear helps create more space for clothes we actually like and want to wear. This allows for better organization and easier access to your favorite wardrobe items.

The clothes we don't wear may be valuable to other people. Donating unused clothes to charities or giving them to someone else can benefit both you and others.

Do a wardrobe check once a year!

54. Choose black underwear

Black underwear is very universal and goes with many different styles and colors of clothing. It can be worn both every day and for special occasions, which makes it very practical.

Black underwear is less susceptible to visible signs of use, such as stains and wear, compared to light colored underwear.

55. Match your socks to your pants

By matching your socks to the color of your pants, you can create a more consistent and harmonious look. Socks that are similar in color to the color of your pants create the appearance of a uniform line, which can make the entire outfit seem more well-thought-out.

Matching socks to the color of your trousers is usually more elegant and discreet, which may be appropriate in more formal or professional situations.

56. Equip yourself with a white T-shirt

A white T-shirt is a classic and suits almost any situation and style. It can be worn both every day and for more formal occasions, it can be combined with jeans, fabric trousers, under a jacket or even under a sweater.

A white T-shirt is easy to combine with other items of clothing. It matches many colors, patterns and styles, which makes creating different styles easier.

The white color is neutral and refreshing. It is perfect for summer styling, reflecting the sun and keeping you cool.

Cotton white T-shirts are usually comfortable, breathable and easy to care for, which makes them a practical wardrobe item.

Equip yourself with several pieces!

57. Buy two pairs of elegant shoes

Brown and black shoes are classics and match many different clothing styles and colors. This makes them suitable for both everyday and more formal occasions.

Brown shoes will look great with clothes in shades of green, brown, beige or navy blue, while black shoes will match many other colors, including gray, navy blue, white or black.

Having two pairs of shoes in different colors will allow you to create more diverse styles. You can match the shoes with the rest of your outfit to achieve the desired visual effect.

High-quality leather shoes, regardless of color, can last for many years, so having two pairs in different colors can be an investment in durable and universal footwear.

Oxford shoes are a great example!

58. Wear sandals correctly

The combination of sandals and socks is often perceived as stylistically inappropriate and may be considered a lack of aesthetics.

Sandals are typically worn on warmer days when the foot has room to breathe, while socks are an item of clothing worn in colder conditions. The combination of these two elements may seem contradictory due to their functions and purpose.

Socks can restrict airflow to the feet and cause discomfort, as well as lead to excessive sweating of the feet. Additionally, wearing sandals without socks allows for better ventilation and foot hygiene.

To summarize, wearing sandals with socks is often considered a fashion faux pas due to the lack of aesthetics, inconsistency with style and violation of fashion rules.

59. Take care of your shoes

Taking care of your shoes regularly is crucial for their durability, appearance and wearing comfort.

Regular maintenance and care of your shoes can significantly increase their durability. Regular cleaning, lubrication and impregnation help protect leather or other materials from external factors such as moisture, dirt and salt.

Well-maintained shoes are usually more comfortable to wear. Regular care can prevent deformation, damage or abrasion, which translates into comfort of use.

Removing dirt and bacteria from the inside of shoes can prevent unpleasant odors and skin infections.

Care should also include sports shoes.

As a result, regular shoe care can contribute to their long-term use, better appearance and greater wearing comfort. Therefore, it is worth spending some time on regular maintenance of your shoes to enjoy them as long as possible.

60. Choose your colors

Combining colors in a men's wardrobe can be a creative process that highlights style and personality while maintaining elegance and consistency.

It's usually a good idea to start by combining classic basic colors such as black, white, gray, navy blue and brown. These are universal colors that are easy to combine and match many other colors.

The contrast between colors can add dynamics and interest to an outfit. For example, a combination of dark and light colors or warm and cool colors can create an interesting visual effect.

Many successful stylings are based on the three-color rule: the main color (e.g. navy blue), an additional color (e.g. gray) and an accent color (e.g. red). This allows you to create a consistent but interesting look.

Neutral colors such as white, black, gray, beige or brown can serve as a basic base to which you can add color accents. They allow for flexible combinations with other colors.

It is worth avoiding an excess of different intense colors in one styling to avoid the effect of colorful excess. Instead, you can choose subtle color accents or plain color combinations with the addition of a single, distinct color.

61. Turn red

The color red is often seen as a color associated with energy, passion and self-confidence. It can have a variety of influences on attractiveness depending on context and interpretation.

Red is an intense and expressive color that can quickly attract attention. This can make a person wearing red clothes more noticeable and attractive to others.

Red is a strong color, and when used properly, it is associated with a higher social class.

The color red can help accentuate your figure and figure, which can further increase your physical attractiveness.

62. Use visual effects

● Black: Black is widely known for slimming the figure. Black T-shirts can visually reduce the size of the body, creating a "drawing" effect on the figure. In addition, black is also elegant and versatile, which makes t-shirts in this color a popular choice for many different occasions.

● White: White T-shirts are bright and visually enlarge the figure. They can give the impression of a larger and more open appearance. Moreover, white T-shirts are also universal and easy to combine with other items of clothing.

● Saturated colors: T-shirts in intense, saturated colors, such as red, blue or green, can attract attention and add energy to the styling. They can also add some dynamism to the figure.

● Pastel colors: T-shirts in pastel colors, such as pink, mint or light blue, are delicate and pleasing to the eye. They can give the look lightness and subtlety.

● Neutral colors: T-shirts in neutral colors such as gray, beige or brown are versatile and easy to pair with other clothes. They can be a good background for more expressive styling accents.

- Stripes and patterns: T-shirts with stripes or other patterns can add an extra dimension to an outfit. Vertical stripes can lengthen the silhouette, while horizontal stripes can widen it.

Please remember that the effect of colors on the figure can be subtle and depends on many factors, such as body shape, body proportions and the way the shirt is worn and styled.

63. Buy 5 suits

When building your suit wardrobe, it's a good idea to start with classic colors that are versatile and suitable for many different occasions. Here are some suit colors worth having in your collection:

- Navy blue: A navy blue suit is an absolute classic and can be worn for more formal occasions as well as business meetings and weddings. It is elegant, universal and always fashionable.

- Gray: A gray suit is also very versatile and goes with many different styles. A light gray suit may be perfect for summer events, while a dark gray suit will work great in a business context.

- Black: A black suit is a classic option for more formal occasions such as evening celebrations or gala events. It is also a popular choice in the business environment.

- Brown: A brown suit, especially in shades of dark brown, can be an elegant and stylish choice for more casual occasions such as parties or dates.

- Beige: A beige suit adds lightness and character to the styling, perfect for summer events and casual meetings.

64. Don't unbutton your jacket while standing

A button-down jacket maintains the proportions and shape of the figure. A properly fitted jacket emphasizes the shoulders and waist, which adds elegance to the entire appearance.

65. Don't button your jacket while sitting

While sitting, a buttoned jacket may wrinkle and deform, which does not look aesthetically pleasing. Unbuttoning the jacket allows you to adjust it more freely to your figure and avoid unwanted folds and wrinkles.

66. Pay attention to the buttons

Wearing a jacket requires knowing a few simple rules.

A single-breasted jacket with two buttons is fastened only with the top button.

A double-breasted jacket is fastened with the middle button or the two top buttons.

A single-breasted jacket with three buttons is fastened with the middle button or the two top buttons.

67. Don't combine a short-sleeved shirt and a jacket

A short-sleeved shirt is usually more casual, while a jacket is more formal and elegant. Combining these two elements can cause a conflict of styles.

68. Don't wear a tie with a short-sleeved shirt

Short shirt sleeves are usually associated with a casual, summer style, while a tie is a symbol of formality. Combining these two elements can lead to a conflict of styles and disproportion.

69. Choose accessories for your suit

Once you have suits in these basic colors, you can start creating a variety of combinations with shirts, ties, shoes and accessories. Here are some tips on how to do it:

- Basic rule: Light shirts go with dark suits, while dark shirts look best with light suits.

- Ties: Choose ties that harmonize with the color of the suit and contrast with the color of the shirt. For example, you can choose a burgundy or gold tie for a navy blue suit with a white shirt.

- Accessories: Add pops of color with accessories such as ties, cufflinks, pocket handkerchiefs and belts. Try to make the accessories match each other and create a coherent style.

- Shoes: Choose shoes that match the character and color of the suit. Typically, black or brown shoes are a safe choice, but you can also experiment with other colors such as burgundy or navy.

It is important to match the style and colors of your outfit to the occasion in which you will wear the suit and to your own taste and personality.

70. Learn to tie a tie

Knowing how to tie a tie adds elegance and professionalism to your appearance. In many business and formal settings, wearing a tie is considered a sign of appropriate dress, and knowing how to tie it correctly can enhance your image

Instruction:

- Start by putting on a shirt and standing in front of a mirror with the tie around your neck, with the wider part of the tie on the left and the narrower part on the right.

- Determine the length of your tie: The longer part of the tie should reach the middle of your waist or be slightly shorter when tied.

- Take the wide part of the tie with your right hand and rub it through the tie knot.

- Fold the right side of the tie over the top of the tie and return it to the right side.

- Take the wide part of the tie with your left hand and rub it through the loop created by folding the right side of the tie.

- Pull the wider part of the tie back through the tie knot, taking care not to make the loop created by folding the right side of the tie too tight.

● Thoroughly knead and straighten the knot by moving it upwards along the tie.

● Finally, gently pull both ends of the tie to adjust the knot to the desired length and position.

● Check in the mirror to make sure the knot is even and well tied.

71. Don't wear a tie that's too long or too short

- The tie should be the right length to match the length of your torso and maintain proportions. A tie that is too long will hang too far below the waist and may look sloppy, while a tie that is too short may seem comical.

- The end of the tie should touch the top of the belt or reach halfway down.

72. Don't unbutton your collar when wearing a tie

A button-down collar can look sloppy and hide the tie, which should be the visual centerpiece when wearing a shirt with a tie. Keeping a neat and fitted collar emphasizes the elegance of the entire outfit.

73. Create 75 fashionable combinations

For this purpose you need:

- 5 suits: black, navy, brown, gray, beige.
- 2 white shirts.
- 2 cream shirts.
- 2 blue shirts.

Ready! This set allows you to freely mix and create a great outfit!

74. Match the color of your shoes

Here are some tips on how to match shoe colors to different types of outfits:

- Black shoes:

o They match formal and elegant outfits such as suits in black, navy blue or gray.

o They can also be worn with some more casual styles such as dark jeans and a shirt, especially in more formal circumstances.

- Brown shoes:

o They match perfectly with brown and beige suits and various shades of gray.

o They also match casual styles such as jeans and a sweater or shirt.

- Brown leather shoes (darker shades):

o Perfect to wear with suits in shades of brown, green, navy blue, jeans and other casual styles.

o They can also work well with more elegant outfits, especially if they have a more classic shape and finish.

- Burgundy shoes:

○ They look good with navy blue and gray suits and with various shades of brown.

○ They can add an interesting color accent to an outfit, especially if worn with neutral colored clothes.

- Beige shoes:

○ Perfect to wear with light suits such as beige, white, light gray, as well as with jeans and other casual styles.

○ They suit more summer and casual occasions, but can also be worn in more formal situations as long as they are made of the right materials and have an elegant look.

○

When choosing the color of shoes to match your outfit, it is also worth paying attention to the style and formality of the occasion in which you will wear the clothes. It is also important that the shoes match the rest of the outfit's colors and create a coherent styling.

75. Choose a headgear

Choosing the perfect headgear for a man depends on several factors, including the occasion, personal style, face shape and preferences.

The first step is to consider the occasion for which you will wear the hat. For example:

- Elegant hats will be appropriate for formal or business meetings.

- For informal outings, such as walking around the city or meeting friends, you can choose a more casual headgear, such as a baseball cap, baseball cap or flat cap.

Choose a headgear that suits your personal style and taste. If you prefer a classic and elegant look, you can choose a hat. If you prefer a more casual and modern style, a baseball cap or baseball cap may be a better choice.

Certain headgear styles may better suit certain face shapes. For example:

- People with a round face may prefer hats that add height, such as hats with a higher body.

- People with an oval face can wear almost any type of headgear because they have proportions that suit most styles.

● People with a square face may want to avoid flat-brimmed headgear, which may accentuate the shape of their face. Instead, they can choose headgear with rounded shapes or wider bodies.

76. Order a custom-made coat

A coat can be a key styling element, adding elegance and sophistication to your entire wardrobe. A properly selected coat can emphasize your personal style and additionally diversify your appearance.

The coat is a protective layer against rain, wind, snow and cold.

A coat is a universal piece of clothing that can be worn on many different occasions - from everyday walks to formal occasions. Thanks to its versatility, it can be combined with both casual and elegant styles.

A coat is a classic element of men's wardrobe that never goes out of fashion. Due to its timeless nature, it can be worn for many seasons, making it a worthwhile investment for the long term.

When you order a coat from a tailor, you will receive a unique product that will not be mass-available in stores. You will be sure that no one else will wear the same coat, which adds uniqueness and individuality to your style.

Short coats are suitable for people of small height, and long coats are dedicated to tall people.

It is worth remembering that short clothes lengthen the figure, and long clothes shorten it!

77. Button up the carcass

Use the visual effect.

Buttoning up a fitted coat or jacket will make you look slimmer!

78. Get help from a stylist

Using a personal stylist can have many benefits for a man, especially when it comes to his appearance and style.

A personal stylist has specialist knowledge of fashion, trends, cuts, colors and proportions. Thanks to this, he can advise on the selection of clothes and accessories that will best suit the client's individual characteristics and preferences.

A personal expert works with the client individually, taking into account his personal preferences, lifestyle, body structure and the goals he wants to achieve. Thanks to this, each styling session is tailored to the specific needs of the client.

Searching for the perfect clothes and creating styles can be time-consuming and frustrating. A personal stylist can save the client time and effort by helping them choose the right clothes and complete outfits faster and more effectively.

Moreover, specialist services are today extremely available and attractive in terms of price.

79. Wear a timeless watch

A timeless watch with an elegant design never goes out of fashion. It is not subject to trends, so it will remain stylish for many years.

Wearing an elegant watch can be an expression of class, style and good taste. A well-chosen watch can emphasize your personality and add self-confidence.

Watches made of high-quality materials, such as stainless steel or gold, can increase in value over time. As a result, purchasing a professional watch can also be a financial investment.

A professional watch can also be a symbol of social status and success. Wearing such a watch can help build the image of a confident and successful person.

80. Take care of your eyesight

Choosing the perfect glasses for a man depends on several factors, such as face shape, lifestyle, personal preferences and current trends.

This aspect applies to prescription glasses, but also to sunglasses.

When choosing glasses, it is worth paying attention to the shape of your face and matching the appropriate type of frames to it. For example:

- If you have a round face, you can choose glasses with angular frames to help balance the round shape.

- For people with a square or rectangular face, glasses with more rounded shapes can soften the sharp lines of the face.

- For an oval face, most glasses shapes can fit, so you can experiment with different styles.

It is also important to take into account the user's lifestyle and needs. For example, if you spend a lot of time doing outdoor activities, it's a good idea to choose glasses with high-quality lenses that will provide protection against UV radiation and other harmful factors.

GLASSES CAN BE USED for various purposes, such as everyday wear, driving, sports or reading. Therefore, it is worth choosing glasses that suit your needs. For example, if you need sunglasses for sports activities, it is worth investing in models that provide stability and good visibility.

The color of your glasses frames should complement the color of your skin, eyes and hair. In general, people with fair skin often look better in light frame colors, while people with darker skin may prefer darker frame colors.

81. Choose a leather wallet

A good leather wallet adds elegance and class to men's clothing. It is an accessory that attracts attention and can emphasize your personal style.

Wallets made of high-quality leather are usually very durable. Unlike wallets made of cheaper materials, leather wallets usually retain their appearance and quality for a long time.

Many people associate leather with luxury and a high standard of living, so owning a leather wallet can add a certain kind of social status to a man's image.

A well-designed leather wallet can help you better organize your money, credit cards, and ID documents

82. Wear a leather belt

Leather belts are usually seen as elegant and stylish clothing accessories. By adding such a belt to his wardrobe, a man can emphasize his taste and attention to appearance.

By choosing a belt made of high-quality leather and solid buckles, a man looks perfect.

A leather belt can perfectly match other items of clothing, such as shoes or a wallet. A matching belt color or texture can add cohesion and harmony to the entire outfit.

Choose a black belt for black shoes and a brown belt for brown shoes.

83. Try suspenders

Suspenders can add elegance and style to an outfit, especially when they are made of high-quality materials and have attractive details.

For those who don't like wearing a belt or want to change their appearance, suspenders can be an attractive alternative that adds originality and character to the outfit.

Suspenders will work well with elegant outfits, but also with looser styles.

It is worth remembering that we do not wear a belt and suspenders at the same time.

Suspenders are dedicated to trousers without belt loops.

84. Wear cufflinks

If you want to stand out or emphasize your individual character, cufflinks will be perfect!

Today, it is an attractive styling accessory that requires the purchase of a special shirt to fasten the accessory.

85. Choose a pocket square

A pocket square is a perfect addition to both elegant and casual styles. The pocket square does not need to be combined with a bow tie or tie.

It is generally accepted that a white pocket square is dedicated to official and formal occasions, and the more colorful forms can be intended for less formal events.

Moreover, the tie and pocket square should be similar in color, but not identical.

Here's a simple way to fold a pocket square using the TV fold method, which will result in a narrow strip sticking out from the chest pocket:

- The first step is to fold our pocket square in half.

- Then we make a few more folds along the shorter side so that the resulting rectangle fits the width of the chest pocket.

The final step is to fold the resulting shape to match the depth of our pocket - the ideal protrusion height is 1 or 1.5 cm.

86. Travel in style

Having a chic leather bag or backpack can bring many benefits, both in terms of style, functionality and prestige.

Leather bags and backpacks are a symbol of elegance and class. By adding such an accessory to your wardrobe, you can elevate your look and look more polished.

High-quality leather bags and backpacks are usually very durable and resistant to wear and tear. Investing in such a bag can therefore be a long-term decision because it will last for many years.

Leather bags and backpacks suit many different clothing styles and occasions. They can be worn both to work and during social gatherings or travel.

87. Take cold showers

A cold shower can stimulate a man, giving him energy and vitality. A lively and energetic person may be perceived as more attractive by others.

Cold showers can also improve blood circulation, which can contribute to better skin appearance and overall health. Although cold showers are not a replacement for proper skin care, they can be part of a healthy skin care routine.

Before implementing this point, you should consult your doctor to eliminate possible contraindications.

88. Quit smoking

Quitting smoking brings a number of health benefits in both the short and long term.

Quitting smoking reduces the risk of respiratory diseases. Breathing ability improves, which translates into better physical performance.

Smoking increases the risk of lung cancer and cardiovascular diseases such as coronary heart disease, heart attack and stroke. Quitting smoking helps to improve the condition of blood vessels and lower blood pressure.

Quitting smoking can have aesthetic benefits, such as improving the appearance of your skin, reducing wrinkles, and reducing the yellow tint of your teeth.

Quitting smoking also brings financial benefits because it eliminates spending on cigarettes.

How to achieve this?

○ State clear reasons why you want to quit smoking. This may be improved health, protection of loved ones against second-hand smoking, financial savings or improvement of general well-being.

○ Choose a specific day when you decide to quit smoking. Try to make it close to the date, but at the same time far enough away to give you time to prepare.

○ Tell your family, friends and colleagues about your decision. Finding support from loved ones can be crucial in difficult times.

○ Consult your doctor or smoking cessation specialist. They can offer support, prescribe medications to help you quit smoking, or refer you to assistance programs.

○ Identify situations that usually make you reach for a cigarette. Prepare for these situations and find alternatives, such as chewing nicotine gum or sipping water.

○ Get rid of cigarettes, ashtrays and other smoking-related items from your surroundings. This can help reduce tempting situations.

○ Choose healthy alternatives that can help minimize the urge to smoke. This could be chewing gum, sucking sugar-free candy or chewing gum.

○ Look for alternative methods of relaxation, such as meditation, yoga or deep breathing. They will help you deal with the stress that often accompanies the process of quitting smoking.

○ Record your progress and celebrate even the smallest successes. This can be motivating and helps keep you engaged in the quitting process.

○ Relapses are part of the quitting process. If you make a mistake, don't give up. Identify what went wrong and focus on continuing your efforts.

89. Create a sleep routine

Going to bed and waking up at the same time regularly can have a number of benefits for your physical and mental health.

The human body has an internal biological clock that regulates the sleep-wake cycle. Regularly going to bed and waking up at the same time helps adjust this clock, which contributes to better sleep.

A regular sleep schedule helps keep your energy and performance stable throughout the day. Fixed sleep hours can counteract the feeling of fatigue and apathy.

This routine makes it easier to get up in the morning and also to fall asleep later. Moreover, we function in a more balanced and mindful way.

Constant sleep hours may affect cognitive functions such as concentration, memory and the ability to solve problems, which translates into effectiveness in carrying out everyday duties, also in the professional sphere.

From today on, I will focus on...

From today I will wake up at...

90. Take advantage of sleep stages

Sleep consists of cycles, called sleep stages, that repeat during one night. Sleep stages are divided into two main categories: REM and NREM.

The sleep cycle begins with NREM (N1,N2,N3) and progresses to REM and then returns to NREM. The entire cycle lasts about 90-120 minutes, and several such cycles are completed in one night.

It is important to go through all stages of sleep because each of them has important functions in the body's regeneration and mental processes.

The basic benefits of sleep according to this strategy include, among others, better physical and mental regeneration, stress reduction, and strengthening of the immune system.

91. Get enough sleep

Getting enough sleep is fundamental to your physical health, mental health and overall well-being.

Sleep is the period during which the body physically regenerates. During this time, tissue repair, strengthening of the immune system, as well as cell growth and regeneration processes take place.

Adequate sleep affects cognitive functions such as concentration, attention, memory and problem-solving ability. Sleep helps consolidate information and consolidate experiences.

Adequate sleep has a huge impact on your overall well-being. People who get regular sleep tend to cope better with stress, are more focused, creative and have better mental well-being.

So how much should you sleep? It is believed that adults should sleep at least 7 hours a day.

92. You are what you eat

Nutrition plays an important role in maintaining the health of your skin, hair and overall body, which in turn can affect your overall attractiveness. Here are some key aspects of nutrition that can help improve your attractiveness:

- Balanced diet: Eating balanced meals containing appropriate amounts of protein, carbohydrates, fats, vitamins and minerals has a beneficial effect on the appearance of the skin and hair. A diet rich in a variety of nutrients supports cellular regeneration and maintains skin elasticity.

- Water: Drinking enough water is crucial to hydration, which has a direct impact on skin elasticity. Well-hydrated skin can look more healthy and radiant.

- Antioxidant-rich foods: Antioxidant-rich foods, such as berries, leafy greens, nuts and seeds, help protect the skin from the harmful effects of free radicals. Antioxidants help fight skin aging processes.

- Omega-3 fatty acids: Foods containing omega-3 fatty acids, such as oily fish, walnuts and flaxseeds, can support skin health by providing adequate hydration and reducing inflammation.

• Protein: Eating enough protein is important for building collagen, which is crucial for skin elasticity. Protein sources such as meat, fish, eggs, legumes and dairy products should be regularly included in your diet.

• Healthy fats: Essential fats, such as those found in avocados, olive oil and nuts, support healthy skin and hair. They provide adequate hydration and support sebum production.

• Avoiding harmful substances: Limiting your intake of harmful substances such as alcohol, smoking or eating highly processed foods can help keep your skin looking healthy.

93. Eat less sweets

Limiting the consumption of sweet snacks and sweetened drinks can bring a number of health benefits, including a positive impact on your appearance. Here are some reasons why limiting your sweet intake may be beneficial:

• Oral health: Excessive sugar consumption can contribute to tooth decay and other dental problems. Limiting sugary snacks helps maintain oral health, which affects the overall appearance of your smile.

• Healthy skin: A diet high in excessive amounts of simple sugars can influence inflammation in the body and contribute to skin problems such as acne. Limiting your intake of sweets can help keep your skin healthy.

• Weight control: Sweetened products are often high in calories and have little nutritional value. Limiting their consumption can help control body weight, which in turn affects the overall appearance of the figure.

• Stabilizing energy levels: Consuming large amounts of simple sugars can lead to rapid increases and decreases in blood glucose levels, which affects energy levels and well-being. Cutting back on sweets can help maintain more stable energy levels.

- Improving skin condition: Too many simple sugars can lead to glycation processes, which can affect skin elasticity and accelerate the aging process. Limiting your sugar intake can help keep your skin healthy and firm.

- Heart health: A diet high in excess sugars may increase the risk of heart disease. Limiting your intake of sweets is recommended as part of a healthy cardiovascular diet.

94. Drink more water

Regularly drinking the right amount of water is important for maintaining health and can have a positive effect on your appearance. Here are some reasons why drinking water is important for your attractiveness and overall health:

- Skin hydration: Water plays a key role in skin hydration. Drinking enough water helps maintain skin elasticity, prevents it from drying out, and may help reduce fine lines and wrinkles.

- Cleansing the body: Water helps remove toxins and impurities from the body, which keeps the skin clean. Drinking enough water supports detoxification processes, which has a beneficial effect on the overall condition of the skin.

- Acne Prevention: Well-hydrated skin is less susceptible to acne. Drinking enough water can help keep your sebum production balanced, which is important for healthy skin.

- Maintaining skin firmness: Water supports the production of collagen, which gives the skin firmness and elasticity. Adequate hydration contributes to maintaining a healthy skin structure.

• Improve skin color: Drinking water can promote healthy skin color, giving it natural radiance and glow. Well-hydrated people often appear more radiant and fresh.

• Healthy hair: Hydration of the body also affects the condition of the hair. Water delivers essential nutrients to the hair follicle, which helps maintain its shine and elasticity.

• Weight management: Drinking water before meals can help stave off hunger, which in turn can help maintain a healthy weight. A healthy weight can affect the attractiveness of your figure.

95. Give up alcohol

Giving up alcohol can have numerous health benefits. Here are some reasons why giving up alcohol can have a positive impact on your attractiveness and overall health:

- Healthy skin: Alcohol can dehydrate the body, which affects the elasticity of the skin. Giving up alcohol and increasing water consumption can improve skin hydration, which will improve its healthy appearance.

- Wrinkle Prevention: Excessive alcohol consumption can accelerate the aging process of the skin and promote the development of wrinkles. Abstinence can help maintain skin firmness.

- Reduce inflammation: Alcohol can cause inflammation in the body, which is associated with various skin problems such as acne and redness. Giving up alcohol can help reduce inflammation.

- Better hydration: Alcohol is a diuretic, which can lead to fluid loss and dehydration. Adequate hydration is crucial for healthy skin, hair and the entire body.

- Improved hair health: Alcohol can affect the health of your hair, making it dry and brittle. Giving up alcohol can help improve the overall condition of your hair.

● Healthier Liver: Alcohol is processed by the liver, and excessive consumption can lead to damage to this organ. A healthy liver is important for the effective removal of toxins from the body, which also affects the overall health of the skin.

It is worth noting that giving up alcohol is an individual decision that depends on many factors, including health, lifestyle and personal preferences. It is always a good idea to consult a health professional when making changes to your diet or lifestyle.

96. Get moving

Regular physical activity, including walking and cycling, not only has health benefits, but also positively affects external attractiveness. Here are some reasons why getting moving can benefit your appearance:

- Healthy skin: Physical activity increases blood flow, which helps deliver more oxygen and nutrients to skin cells. This can contribute to healthier-looking and radiant skin.

- Improved circulation: Regular walking and cycling promote blood circulation, which in turn can contribute to better skin elasticity and overall circulatory health.

- Maintaining a healthy weight: Regular physical activity helps maintain a healthy weight. A healthy weight affects body proportions, which can have a positive impact on the attractiveness of the figure.

- Stress reduction: Physical activity helps in reducing stress levels. Stress can negatively impact the appearance of your skin, accelerating the aging process, and can also cause skin problems such as acne and redness.

- Improving overall fitness: Regular physical activity supports the overall health of the body. People who are in good physical condition often appear more energetic, which can have a positive effect on their overall appearance.

• Maintaining muscle flexibility: Walking and cycling engage different muscle groups, which helps keep them flexible and supple. This affects the overall appearance of the figure.

• Better well-being: Physical activity releases endorphins, called happiness hormones. This has a positive effect on your overall well-being and can affect your self-confidence, which is also important for attractiveness.

How to start?

• Find your motivation: Determine why you want to start exercising at home. Is the goal to improve fitness, maintain health, reduce stress or lose weight? Motivation will help you stay regular.

• Select type of activity: Select the type of physical activity that interests you and which will be adapted to your skills. It can be yoga, strength training, dancing, cardio exercises or even short walks.

• Organize the space: Prepare an exercise area in your home. This can be a piece of free floor where you can move comfortably. Also try to create a pleasant environment, for example by playing your favorite music.

• Get the necessary equipment: Some activities require minimal equipment, such as yoga mats, dumbbells, resistance bands, etc. Depending on what you choose, you can customize your equipment.

● Start with easy exercises: If you're just starting out, don't do it at the highest intensity level right away. Choose easier exercises and gradually increase the intensity as your fitness improves.

● Establish a regular schedule: Plan your training sessions so that they are a regular part of your week. Regularity is key to achieving results.

● Find support: Exercise with a friend, family or use online sources of motivation such as online training videos or mobile apps.

● Be flexible: Physical activity at home can be adapted to changes in your life. If something doesn't work, try something new. The most important thing is to keep activity as a regular part of everyday life.

● Be patient and have fun with it: Results are not always immediate, so be patient. It is important to enjoy the process itself and feel the joy of physical activity.

Remember, it's always a good idea to consult your doctor before starting a new training program, especially if you have any existing health problems.

97. Practice martial arts

Martial arts and self-defense teach effective defense techniques that can be extremely useful in situations of threat or attack. Having such knowledge and skills gives you self-confidence and a sense of security.

Martial arts training requires self-discipline. Regular practice allows a man to develop these qualities, which can have a positive impact on many other areas of life, such as work, education and relationships with others.

Martial arts training allows you to improve your physical condition, strength and flexibility. A strong body is as important as the mind, so regular physical activity can help a man be healthier and more energetic.

Martial arts teach techniques for breathing control, relaxation and stress management. Thanks to this, a man can better cope with life's difficulties and challenges while remaining calm and composed.

Martial arts training often takes place in a group, which helps build relationships with other people. Working with training partners and instructors can help a man develop interpersonal skills and build new friendships.

98. Build muscle

Strong and well-defined muscles can add physical attractiveness by emphasizing body proportions, improving posture, and overall appearing strong and healthy.

People with a strong and muscular body structure often show greater self-confidence and a positive attitude towards themselves. Building muscle can increase your self-esteem and confidence, which may be attractive to others.

Training and developing muscles together can be a form of building social relationships and common interests.

99. Strengthen your neck

Strengthening your neck can be an extremely important element in shaping your attractiveness.

A thicker neck can affect body proportions, which some people find attractive. Increased neck musculature can create an impression of strength and physical harmony.

The training is extremely simple but effective.

- Lie on the edge of the bed face up so that your neck sticks out.

- Lower your head position and then raise your head to the starting position.

100. Exercise your forearms

Forearm exercises can help build muscle strength and endurance, which is crucial in performing everyday activities and sports.

Showing off the muscles of the forearms can add aesthetics to the figure, especially if it is proportional to the rest of the body. Well-developed forearms can accentuate your overall figure and physical appearance.

To sum up, forearm exercises can bring many benefits, including building strength and endurance, improving the aesthetics of the figure, strengthening stabilizing muscles and improving functionality.

101. Laugh

A daily dose of laughter is of great importance for physical and mental health.

Laughter has a positive impact on physical health by stimulating the immune system, improving blood circulation, lowering stress levels and reducing muscle tension.

Laughter also helps us look at life from perspective, which can improve our well-being and ability to cope with difficulties.

A regular dose of laughter makes life more joyful and fulfilling. Laughter allows us to enjoy the moment and appreciate the small pleasures of everyday life. This is especially important in the face of life's challenges and difficulties - and there are plenty of them.

A sense of humor is a very important ingredient of attractiveness!

102. Head high

Holding your head high conveys self-confidence and self-acceptance. People usually perceive people who maintain a straight posture and raise their head as more confident and decisive.

A head held high can be a sign of strength of character and determination. People who maintain a confident and decisive attitude are often perceived as more reliable and competent.

This posture also allows you to expose the jawline and cheekbones, which is especially important in the context of attractiveness.

103. Look into the eyes

Looking into the eyes during a conversation helps to establish and maintain contact with the other person. This signals that you are focused and engaged in what the other person is saying.

Looking into the eyes during a conversation can build trust between interlocutors. This is proof of respect and openness to the other person, which contributes to better communication and interpersonal relationships.

People who look confidently in the eye during a conversation seem more confident and decisive. This is a signal that you trust yourself and your communication skills.

People who maintain eye contact while talking are often perceived as more attractive and confident. This positive impression can contribute to building positive relationships with other people.

Eye contact should be maintained for approximately 70% of the conversation.

104. Take care of your body language

Be aware of your posture and continually restore it to the right state to build a healthy habit.

Gestures that are too abrupt or chaotic may express uncertainty. Try to maintain controlled and balanced movements that add confidence to your movement.

Remember that your posture represents your feelings, but can also shape them - keep your posture straight to gain self-confidence.

- Standing: Stand straight, keep your head high, your chest slightly up, your back straight, and your arms hanging by your body. The position is wide and stable. Avoid slouching, rolling your shoulders, or keeping your arms in your pockets or crossed over your chest. A straight posture expresses self-confidence and a positive attitude. Do not cross your arms or feet.

- Sitting: open body communication without crossing arms or legs. Don't hide your hands or cover your eyes.

- Moving: Don't hesitate when moving, have decisive steps and aim forward. Slow, confident movements make you appear more confident and decisive.

105. Use matching and mirroring

These effective methods involve very subtle, thoughtful and skillful imitation of the interlocutor's behavior

Matching is based on copying movements with the same side, while mirroring is based on the opposite side - then the interlocutor has the impression that he or she is in front of a mirror.

The effectiveness of the methods results from the subconscious search for similarities in our interlocutor.